REX CONWAY'S
SOUTHERN
STEAM JOURNEY
VOLUME ONE

Other books by Rex Conway:

Rex Conway's Steam Album
Rex Conway's Western Steam Journey
Rex Conway's Midland Steam Journey Volume One
Rex Conway's Midland Steam Journey Volume Two
Rex Conway's GWR Album
Rex Conway's Eastern Steam Journey Volume One
Rex Conway's Eastern Steam Journey Volume Two

First published 2010

The History Press
The Mill, Brimscombe Port
Stroud, Gloucestershire, GL5 2QG
www.thehistorypress.co.uk

British Library Cataloguing in Publication Data.
A catalogue record for this book is available from the British Library.

ISBN 978 0 7524 5757 4
Typesetting and origination by The History Press
Printed in Malta.
Manufacturing managed by Jellyfish Print Solutions Ltd

Contents

Introduction

The *Southern Steam Journeys Volume One* and *Two* will be the last of my journeys by steam. We will have covered England and Wales from Penzance in the far west, to Carlisle and Newcastle near the Scottish borders. There was a slight criticism of my journeys by one railway magazine, and it was small, but I would like to respond. The critic felt there was not enough information given in some of the captions, which was deliberate on my part. There are hundreds of books full of information on every class of engine, and I did not want to bore my readers with masses of technical detail. I would rather they opened my books, saw black and white photographs and were taken back to the days when they packed their sandwiches and cameras and went to a station or the lineside and spent a day waiting to see the next train hoping it would be a cop. While accepting that today's colour photographs that appear in

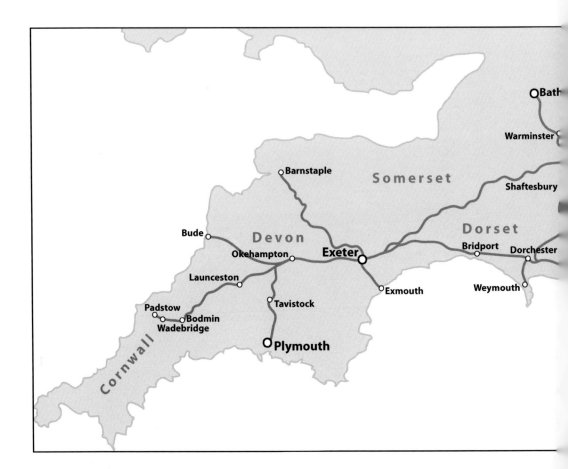

magazines look very good, it seems that a great deal of the quality is done by computer. I do not condemn this as I am hopeless with a laptop, but for me, standing by the lineside in the 1950s waiting for the next train and having to make sure I picked my spot to take one good picture, can never be replaced with a computer or a camera that will take many pictures that can be viewed instantly. If the reader, by opening my books and seeing black and white photographs, is transported back to Steam Days, and in his or her mind relives those steamy days, I feel I have done what I set out to do.

Rex Conway, 2010

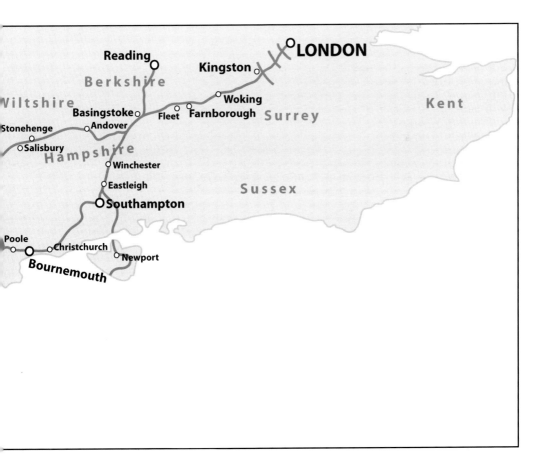

London-bound is 'West Country' 4–6–2 no. 34015 *Exmouth* leaving Bournemouth Central in 1957.

Rex Conway's Southern Steam Journey

ere we are again about to undertake another of my journeys, this one the penultimate, *Southern Steam Journey Volume One*. It started as the final, but one look at the *Railway Atlas* proved it would be impossible to do a Southern journey in one, as the Southern goes in two directions, westward to the holiday destinations of Dorset, Devon and Cornwall, also Reading and the major seaport of Southampton, and the Isle of Wight. The second volume goes in the opposite direction to the south coast, Portsmouth and Brighton taking in the most of the English Channel holiday haunts so familiar to Londoners, then around the Kent Coast and back to London.

On leaving Waterloo, which is where we start our journey, there will not be any of the group sitting down – it will be noses pressed to windows in the compartment, or out in the corridors, with the door windows open. I am sure fellow enthusiasts reading this will be able to recall memories of journeys they have made, and will be able to relate to our Southern journey. On leaving Waterloo, there seem to be trains everywhere, many of them electric, but we are only interested in steam. It seems no sooner have we left Waterloo than we are picking up speed and through Vauxhall where many cricket enthusiasts have de-trained to attend a match at the Oval. Through Vauxhall there are masses of lines; we are now into Clapham, one of the busiest railway junctions in the world. Through Clapham it becomes a little quieter as the main line from Victoria has diverged and is making its way to the south coast. And we are now on our way westwards. We shall be filling our notebooks with numbers, cameras will be clicking merrily at Eastleigh sheds, and then we shall be at the seaside. Through Southampton, next comes the New Forest, famous for its ponies, and then Bournemouth. At Battledown we will be truly heading westwards to Salisbury, Exeter and Plymouth, and then the final leg into Cornwall, reaching Bude, Wadebridge and finally Padstow where we shall be resting our weary bodies. Once again I invite you to join our band of enthusiasts; just make sure you bring your cameras. Welcome aboard!

A classic scene at a 1930s main line station is this view of a little boy looking at the footplate of SR 4–6–0 no. 862 *Lord Collingwood* at Waterloo. Could his thoughts be, 'I want to be an engine driver one day'?

Waterloo, named after the famous battle, was originally sited at Nine Elms, several miles from its present site near the centre of London. Opened in 1839 to serve the London & Southampton Railway (L&SR), it was soon realised that the site was not a good choice on which to build a London terminus. Within ten years it was moved to its present location, no doubt destroying many homes in the process. By 1860 it had been extended again, various bits and pieces were added making it one of the most confusing stations in London. By the turn of the century, the directors of the London & South Western Railway (L&SWR) – the company now working out of Waterloo, travelling to the West of England – had decided that the time had come to sort out the chaos of Waterloo, and enlarge it at the same time. Powers were sought to carry out the work, and these powers were granted, regardless of the fact that many roads would disappear and thousands of people would lose their homes. The station in its present form was completed in 1922, when Queen Mary performed the opening ceremony. It has a huge glazed roof covering twenty-one platforms. The main entrance, the Victory Arch, leads into the concourse where there are dining rooms and several bars. In 1913 in the Long Bar you could obtain a five-course meal for 3s 6d. Waterloo is London's principal station serving Portsmouth, Southampton and Bournemouth as well as many seaside destinations in Devon and Cornwall.

Southern Railway 'Paddlebox' 4–6–0 no. 462 simmering gently waiting for the guard's whistle at Waterloo.

Not the most glamorous job, working empty stock back into a main line station, but to quote a well-worn expression, 'someone has got to do it.' Empty stock for main line trains out of Waterloo can be brought from as far out as Clapham, at least the crew of the tanks drawing these carriages worked right up to the buffer stops at the main concourse, and could be there for half an hour – plenty of time to buy a newspaper, and perhaps finish off the sandwiches and tea they had brought from home, before they feel the main line engine back on at the head of the train. The fireman will now disconnect the train heating pipe and also the brake pipe, so that their loco is free of the carriages. Next, the train loco at the head of carriages blows its hooter, the guard blows his whistle and our small tank engine that brought the train into the platform responds with its whistle; the train is off on its journey. The small tank engine will help get the train started by pushing until it gets to the end of the platform, and there it will part company with the main train and proceed to the carriage department to start all over again.

Standard class 2–6–2 3MT no. 82024, bringing empty stock for a Bournemouth train into Waterloo.

Opposite, top: Class M7 no. 30039 also bringing empty stock into Waterloo.

Opposite, bottom: A 'Paddlebox' at Waterloo in the late 1940s carrying its British Railway number, 30461, on the bufferbeam.

Two night views at Waterloo.

'Merchant Navy' 4–6–2 no. 35017 *Belgian Marine* bringing 'The Bournemouth Belle' into Waterloo at the end of its journey in March 1952.

Another arrival at Waterloo in 1952 is 'West Country' 4–6–2 no. 34011 *Tavistock*.

Just backed down onto its train to Bournemouth is 'West Country' 4–6–2 no. 34004 *Yeovil*. It has made its way to Waterloo from Nine Elms depot. We are reminded at this point by one of our band of enthusiasts that no. 34004 was one of the locos that took part in the 1948 exchange trials where locos were tried on foreign lines – no. 34004 went to Scotland. One can only imagine the surprise on spotters' faces when a Southern Region Spam Can appeared in such places as Aberdeen and Perth.

We are being a little nostalgic now, as no-one in our group is old enough to remember much about the early 1930s when these photographs were taken. We can only envy the enthusiasts of those days who thronged the platforms at Waterloo.

Ready to leave Waterloo is T9 4–4–0 SR no. 284 in about 1930.

Also about to leave Waterloo in about 1930 is a double-headed train hauled by M7 4–4–0T no. 32. The train engine is 'Schools' class 4–4–0 no. 924 *Haileybury*.

Our third nostalgic look at the past is L12 4–4–0 no. 432, again in about 1930, with a plume of steam from the safety valve. The driver is waiting only for the guard's whistle and they will be off.

Still making maximum use of our cameras, our group is trying to make sure we get a photograph of every steam loco, although on a large station like Waterloo it is almost impossible to get a perfect picture every time. We manage to get another couple of nice views but we have now reached that point which all travelling enthusiasts will recognise: the reluctant move from your vantage point at the end of the platform to where the carriages will stop and you can quickly board and hopefully obtain an empty compartment.

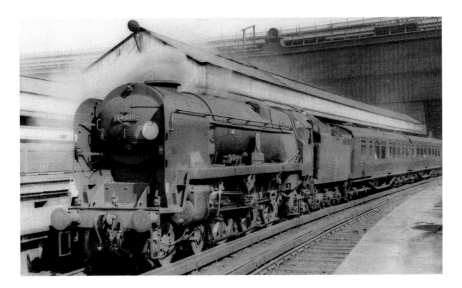

'West Country' 4–6–2 no. 34016 *Bodmin* ready to leave Waterloo.

On its way, 'Merchant Navy' no. 35021 *New Zealand Line* starts out of Waterloo with 'The Royal Wessex'. Originally non-stop to Bournemouth, a distance of 108 miles, there weren't any water troughs on this route, so the enginemen had to be careful not to run dry. Now the train makes several stops so running dry is no longer a problem.

We have found an empty compartment in the first carriage next to the engine, our favourite place on our journeys. It was empty but with our group, plus shoulder bags for books, cameras and (almost as important) our sandwiches, drinks, cakes, bars of chocolate and anything else that railway enthusiasts fill their bags with, we soon fill the compartment, which will be enough to put off any normal traveller from joining us. There goes the guard's whistle and we are off on our Southern journey!

4–6–2 rebuilt 'Merchant Navy' no. 35028 *Clan Line* starts us on our way out of Waterloo.

Working hard at the head of our train is a 'Merchant Navy'. There is quite a climb out of Waterloo, but very quickly we are approaching Vauxhall station which many cricket enthusiasts will know as being the nearest main line station to the Kennington Oval cricket ground. The Oval, home of Surrey Cricket Club, started life in 1844. It was a market garden owned by the Duchy of Cornwall who granted a lease to use it for club cricket. The ground is still leased from the Duchy of Cornwall, and has grown many times in size while the market garden has disappeared.

Double-headed M7s work a train of empty stock out of Waterloo through Vauxhall. The lead engine is no. 30241.

'Schools' 4–4–0 no. 30911 *Dover* working light engine from Nine Elms back to Waterloo, passing through Vauxhall.

Two more views at Vauxhall of expresses on their way westwards. Being British, on hearing the word Vauxhall you immediately think of the former British car company. However, the name is far older than the autombolies, it actually dates back to King John in the fifteenth century, when some of his mercenaries lived in a mansion called 'Faulkes Hall'. Gradually, down the years, this became 'Vauxhall'.

'Remembrance' N15X class 4–6–0 no. 32327 *Trevithick* makes its way through Vauxhall in the early 1950s.

H2 Atlantic 4–4–2 no. 32421 *South Foreland* approaching Vauxhall station with a westbound express in 1949.

Two more early views at Vauxhall.

'Paddlebox' 4–6–0 no. 30461 approaches the platform at Vauxhall in 1949.

H15 4–6–0 no. 30482 approaches the platform at Vauxhall in 1954.

Vauxhall station is a wonderful vantage point for obtaining photographs of expresses making for the holiday destinations of the West with almost non-stop traffic and light engine movements from Nine Elms that back onto carriages at Waterloo. Then, of course, there are the M7s, etc. taking empty stock into Waterloo – and then there comes the noise behind the real reason that seasoned enthusiasts are waiting with cameras poised, the sound of an express approaching.

S15 4–6–0 no. 30512 approaching the platform at Vauxhall.

'King Arthur' 4–6–0 no. 30797 *Sir Blamor de Ganis* approaching Vauxhall.

'Britannia' class 4–6–2 no. 70009 *Alfred the Great* with the Down 'Bournemouth Belle'.

While we will now be leaving Vauxhall, we still have our noses pressed against the windows, cameras poised and notebooks ready, as we shall be passing Nine Elms shed, although you can't see much of the shed from the carriage windows. However, there are always light engine movements to see.

Vauxhall station with 4–6–2 'Merchant Navy' no. 35014 *Nederland Line* roaring through.

Leaving Vauxhall and the capital behind is 'Lord Nelson' 4–6–0 *Howard of Effingham*.

A last view of Vauxhall with 4–6–2 'Merchant Navy' no. 35006 *Peninsular and Oriental S.N. Co.*

We are passing the site of the original terminal station of the London & Southampton Railway which opened in 1839, but a few years later was moved to its permanent site, the Waterloo we know today. The site was then developed as a works and locomotive shed, although the L&SWR deployed its works to Eastleigh. Nine Elms is the principal shed which supplies locomotives for trains out of Waterloo.

'King Arthur' 4–6–0 no. 30772 *Sir Percivale* on shed in 1957.

'King Arthur' 4–6–0 no. 448 *Sir Tristram* photographed on Nine Elms shed in Southern Railway days prior to the Second World War.

'Lord Nelson' class 4–6–0 no. 30859 *Lord Hood* on Nine Elms shed in 1960.

Another view on Nine Elms shed is 'Remembrance' N15X class 4–6–0 no. 32328 *Hackworth*.

'Remembrance' N15X
class 4–6–0 no. 32333
Remembrance on Nine
Elms shed in 1950.

E4 0–6–2T no. 32563
resting at Nine Elms
shed in 1959. This was
the type of loco used
to work empty stock to
and from Waterloo.

2–6–0 U class no. 31634
with an empty tender.
It has probably just
arrived from Waterloo
after working a train
into the capital.

Class T9 4–4–0 no. 30285 at Nine Elms in June 1953. This class of loco was built in 1899 and designed by Drummond for the London & South Western.

When in 1948 the four companies became British Railways, it was decided to hold trials of various locos on different lines. This was to evaluate their successes and shortcomings with a view to designing a standard class for BR that could work anywhere on their system. This view is of no. 35019 *French Line CGT* being prepared for a main line test run to the West Country, at Old Oak Common in 1948.

There is still no chance of taking our seats and relaxing for a few moments. We have now passed Nine Elms and can see Battersea power station and the line from Victoria; or should I say lines, for whichever way you look there is a maze of tracks going from Victoria to Portsmouth and the south-east coast as well as the numerous lines that we are travelling, from Waterloo westwards. Throw in a few freight lines and it can only mean one thing: we are approaching one of the busiest railway junctions in the world – Clapham.

'King Arthur' 4–6–0 no. 30768 *Sir Balin* ready for duty at Stewarts Lane.

4–4–0 'Schools' class no. 30921 *Shrewsbury* on the turntable at Longhedge in 1960.

We are fast approaching Clapham Junction but there is just time for one of our friends to read out from a book he has brought with him that gives some historical information about Clapham. He tells us that it was the first station out of Nine Elms and originally named Wandsworth. In 1846 the name was changed to Clapham Common and it took another fifteen years to acquire the world famous name, Clapham Junction. It is almost unique in having two major railways converging on the station, the London Brighton & South Coast Railway, and the London & South Western Railway. The London Chatham & Dover Railway as well as the Great Western Railway also had running rights through the station. At this point our friend gave up reading from his book as we were just about to pass under the signal-box and hundreds of signals that control the junction, it was time for looking – not talking!

'The Royal Wessex' headed by 'West Country' 4–6–2 no. 34095 *Brentnor*.

'Merchant Navy' 4–6–2 no. 35024 *East Asiatic Company* passing under the signal-box and signals bridge that all enthusiasts will recognise.

T9 4–4–0 no. 30721 shunting stock in Clapham carriage sidings, 1954.

An express headed by 'King Arthur' 4–6–0 no. 30748 *Vivien* making for Waterloo through Clapham.

Three more views at Clapham Junction, a station that trainspotters and railway photographers dream of. Leaving aside the electric trains which are constant, there is still plenty of steam activity.

U class 2–6–0 no. 31798 working its way through Clapham Junction in 1958.

'King Arthur' no. 30742 *Camelot* bringing empty stock into the carriage sidings at Clapham.

L1 4–4–0 no. 31788 making its way through Clapham.

M7 no. 30123 working empty Pullman cars through Clapham on its way to Waterloo to form 'The Bournemouth Belle', introduced in 1931 by the Southern Railway. It ran on Sundays only until 1936 when it became a daily service.

This picture of 'King Arthur' no. 30767 *Sir Valence* at Clapham, is a bit of a mystery. It has a train of fourteen Pullman coaches. If it's heading a train to Bournemouth then it must be the heaviest load of Pullmans ever hauled by a 'King Arthur'. If, on the other hand, it's bringing empty stock from Waterloo to Clapham, what train was worked into Waterloo made up of fourteen cars?

H16 4–6–2T no. 30519 on its way back to Feltham running light through Clapham. Built in 1921 by Urie for the L&SWR, it was one of the heaviest tank engines to run on the rails of any of Britain's railway companies. Coming in at nearly 100 tons, it was an ideal loco for working freight in and out of Feltham's large goods yards.

Passing through Clapham Junction in 1959 is U class 2–6–0 no. 31635, heading for Waterloo.

'West Country' 4–6–2 no. 34006 *Bude* running light engine at Clapham Junction.

H15 4–6–0 no. 30333 heads a train through Clapham. This class was introduced in 1914 by Urie. To my eye this was a powerful-looking engine, spoilt by a silly little chimney.

'Remembrance' N15X class no. 32328 *Hackworth* working westwards through the London suburbs.

T9 no. 313 in Southern days, photographed at Richmond in the early 1930s.

We are reminded that the huge marshalling yards at Feltham are not far from our route westwards. The yards are approximately 15 miles from Waterloo on the Clapham–Reading line. Built shortly after the First World War for the L&SWR, it was controlled by all-electric signal-boxes. It had some sixty lines with several humps, and shunting began in 1921. The G16 4–8–0s and H16 4–6–2Ts were built at Eastleigh especially for hump shunting at Feltham, and working transfer freight trains to other yards in the London area.

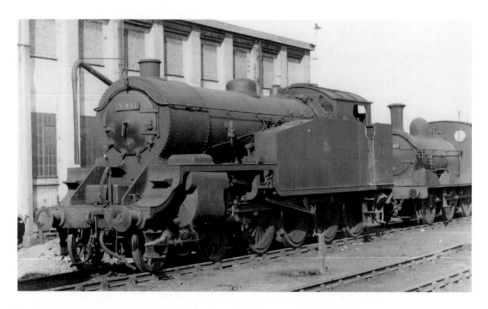

G16 4–8–0T no. 30493 photographed at Feltham in September 1958.

H16 4–6–2T no. 30516 also at Feltham in 1957.

Class Q1 0–6–0 no. 33012 was a revolutionary design by Bulleid as a wartime 'Austerity' locomotive. It was an unusual design but very successful. It is photographed here at Feltham.

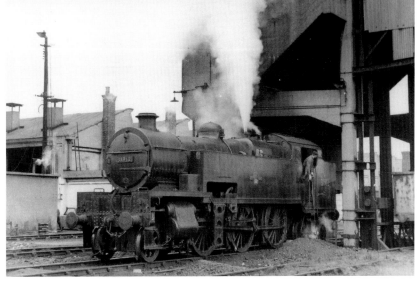

W class 2–6–4T was introduced in 1931 to a Maunsell design. Weighing over 90 tons, it was an ideal freight loco which was also to be seen often on local passenger work.

0–6–0 class 700 no. 30339 introduced in 1897 by Drummond for the L&SWR, seen in the yard at Feltham.

N class 2–6–0 no. 31850 double-headed with a 'West Country' 4–6–2 on a special. Regrettably the location is a bit vague, the only information being that it's near Feltham.

Here are two pre-war views taken somewhere in the suburbs of London. Again, there's very little information as to where the photographs were taken, the only information with the negatives apart from the numbers of the locos was '1935'.

Southern Railway 4–4–0 no. 419.

Another 4–4–0, no. 422. If anyone recognises the locations I would be pleased to hear from them.

Another view in the suburbs of London, no. 31223 C class 0–6–0 heading a freight train, possibly on its way to Feltham.

We are now picking up speed and can relax for a while. We have left Clapham behind with all its activity, passed the junction for Wandsworth which the Victoria–Brighton trains take, then through Earlsfield before approaching Wimbledon.

U class 2–6–0 no. 31620 approaching Wimbledon.

Class N15 'King Arthur' 4–6–0 no. 454 *Queen Guinevere* near Wimbledon in the 1930s.

Now we are passing through Wimbledon known to most people as the home of tennis. The All England Lawn Tennis and Croquet Club, to give it its full title, was founded in 1868. In 1877 the first lawn tennis championship was played here and it is still a yearly event, and considered by many to be the most prestigious event in the tennis calendar. It is also the oldest tennis club in the world, as is the railway, originally called the Surrey Iron Railway, which was the first public carrying railway. The title was changed to the Wimbledon & Croydon Railway, and no doubt has carried millions of tennis fans to this historic club over many years, and is still continuing to do so.

'Lord Nelson' 4–6–0 no. 30858 *Lord Duncan* approaches Wimbledon station with a Plymouth train in 1958.

The original station at Wimbledon was called Wimbledon and Merton and was opened in 1838 by The L&SWR. This station was replaced by a second Wimbledon and Merton in 1881 a short distance away. This station was closed in 1909 and the present station opened on the site of the 1838 station on the same date in 1909.

'King Arthur' 4–6–0 no. 30753 *Melisande* passing Wimbledon A signal-box.

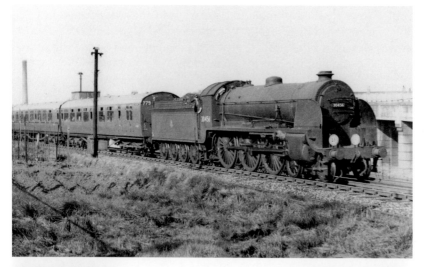

No. 30456, a well-known name in the 'King Arthur' class, *Sir Galahad* photographed in Wimbledon in May 1953.

Entering Wimbledon station is Standard class 5MT no. 73110.

Class T9 no. 30702 with a Waterloo–Southampton train. These 4–4–0s were very successful and have given long service. They first started work in 1899, and are still working hard.

A 1947 view of 'Merchant Navy' no. SR 21C3 *Royal Mail*, an example of the short-lived numbering introduced by Mr Bulleid that confused everybody. It is seen heading a Plymouth-bound train in the outer suburbs of London. These locos also carried a Southern Railway roundel on the smokebox door.

Also leaving London with a westbound express is 'Battle of Britain' no. 21C152 *Lord Dowding*.

Another view in the outer suburbs of London is 'Merchant Navy' no. SR 21C12 *United States Line*, also photographed in 1947.

A few years later in the early 1950s is this view of 'Merchant Navy' no. 35016 *Elders Fyffes* at the head of a westbound express.

Surbiton is now rapidly approaching so at this point I give the floor to one of my fellow enthusiasts who knows more about station history than the rest of us put together. He tells us that the first station was called Surbiton and Kingston and was opened by the L&SWR in July 1863. This name only lasted a few years, for in 1867 it became simply Surbiton. In 1937 it was decided to do a complete rebuild at the same time as the lines were being electrified so the station was completely remodelled in a 1930s look, easily mistaken for an Odeon Cinema, which many locals called it.

'Remembrance' N15X class 4–6–0 no. 32329 *Stephenson* awaits departure at Surbiton station.

Two views of Urie's H16 heavyweight freight tank engines weighing in at 96 tons. They were used extensively for working long freight trains to and from Feltham.

H16 4–6–2T no. 30518 passing through Surbiton.

There are only five locos in the H16 class. This is another view of one of these heavyweight engines, no. 30520, in almost the same spot as the top view.

We now have two 'Lord Nelsons' posed at Surbiton, both waiting for the green from the electric signal at the end of the platform.

'Lord Nelson' 4–6–0 no. 30863 *Lord Rodney* ready to continue its journey after stopping at Surbiton.

Another 'Lord Nelson' waiting to continue its journey after stopping at Surbiton to pick up more passengers is no. 30864 *Sir Martin Frobisher*.

Surbiton was a busy station for steam, being on the main line for expresses to the West Country and also the many trains to Southampton and Bournemouth.

'King Arthur' 4–6–0 no. 30752 *Linette* about to leave Surbiton.

L12 4–4–0 no. 30434 arriving at Surbiton.

'West Country' 4–6–2 no. 34106 *Lydford* has received the green light and is pulling away from Surbiton.

After Surbiton, life as a railway enthusiast will settle down for a time, and we can enjoy a sandwich and a drink, and compare notes about what we have seen on our hectic journey from Waterloo.

Another 'King Arthur' approaching Surbiton, this time it's no. 30780 *Sir Persant*.

Another 'Remembrance' N15X class waiting at Surbiton is no. 32332 *Stroudley*. The fireman has the fire well built up as the safety valve is sending a lot of steam skywards.

'Lord Nelson' no. 30857 *Lord Howe* coming to a halt at Surbiton.

We now have the green light at Surbiton and are on our way again. Very shortly we shall be at Hampton Court Junction, where a short spur to the right leads to Hampton Court, royal home of Henry VIII. It is one of the most popular attractions in Britain, and the terminus at the end of this branch line, built for the L&SWR in 1849, was designed by Sir William Tite, and is certainly a station worthy of a royal residence.

Class D15 4–4–0 no. 30467, introduced in 1912 to a Drummond design for the LS&WR, is photographed approaching Surbiton.

Immediately after the branch for Hampton Court is another junction to the left for Leatherhead and within a few minutes we are approaching Esher at something like 60mph. Esher station is very near to the famous racecourse of Sandown. The first races were held here in the nineteenth century, but it was closed in the 1930s. After the Second World War it was reopened as a horse racing course, and in the 1960s a car racing circuit was built around the site with many famous names such as Stirling Moss going on to hurtle around the track.

Esher West signal-box, photographed on Boxing Day 1949.

'Merchant Navy' 4–6–2 no. 35013 *Blue Funnel* at Esher in 1959.

'Battle of Britain' 4–6–2 no. 34066 *Spitfire* at the head of a special boat train of Pullman coaches near Weybridge, on its way to Southampton docks.

Just beyond Weybridge is a junction which leads north through Virginia Water. Originally this line terminated at Chertsey, but a public outcry persuaded the directors of the L&SWR to extend the line to Virginia Water and into Reading.

N class 2–6–0 no. 31867 has just arrived in Reading station with a train via Virginia Water, waiting for the signal to proceed to Reading South shed 70E.

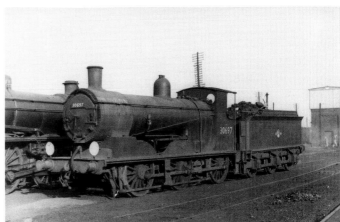

700 class 0–6–0 no. 30697 on Reading South shed in 1953.

'Remembrance' N15X class 4–6–0 no. 32331 *Beattie* receiving last-minute checks on Reading South shed 70E early in 1950.

Photographed near Reading is U class 2–6–0 no. 31618 with only four coaches, suggesting it's a local working.

H15 no. 30524 near Reading with a parcels train.

Things have settled down in our compartment as we pass through the junction at Byfleet into a lovely rural landscape. The trees and bridges are flashing past in the sunshine and our loco sounds in fine form. Once more, our notebooks are out, while we have another sandwich. We compare notes to make sure we agree no mistakes have been made in our jottings, perform another check on the cameras to ensure they are still functioning properly, sit back on the cushions, relax and watch the scenery go by. Apart from stations, there will not be any hectic activity until Eastleigh and Southampton.

T9 4–4–0 no. 281 near Woking in Southern days.

U1 no. 31891 heading a Portsmouth Harbour train near Woking.

We are now through Woking having passed the junction for Guildford on our left – the route the Portsmouth trains take.

....

H16 4–6–2T no. 30517 on Guildford shed.

Another view at Guildford of class H15 no. 30331, a 4–6–0 built in 1914 by Urie for the L&SWR.

Three more views at Guildford shed.

B4 0–4–0T no. 30086 *Havre*. This was an Adams design of 1891 for the L&SWR, especially for working in the docks, shunting on the tight curves that abound in all ports.

Another 0–4–0, even smaller than the B4 above, is no. 30458 *Ironside*, weighing in at just over 21 tons. It was introduced in 1890 for the Southampton Docks Company, which was absorbed into the L&SWR in 1892.

Class E4 0–6–2T no. 32490, a Billington design for the London, Brighton & South Coast Railway in 1910.

A flashback to the 1930s with this view of Southern Railway no. 70, a 4–4–0, near Woking.

Another main line view sees 'Battle of Britain' 4–6–2 no. 34081 *92 Squadron* with a train bound for Southampton. This view is near Brookwood. From Waterloo the line has been gradually rising, which has been fairly hard work for the crew. At Brookwood, the line levels off and falls nearly all the way to Southampton. This gives the crew an easier time with perhaps a spare moment for a cup of tea and a bacon sandwich cooked on the shovel!

We shall soon be passing through another junction at Pirbright, but before we get there I feel we should mention Brookwood in more detail. In 1859 an entrepreneur, Mr George Rastrick, bought 2,000 acres of land that was beside the railway from Woking to Brookwood. This land was already being used to bury London's dead. William Tite was asked to design a station which would be attached to the L&SWR station of Waterloo with an entrance from Westminster Bridge Road. The coffins could be carried from the road to the platform where they could be placed straight onto the train, and the mourners could also board. After a 50-minute journey, the train would arrive at Brookwood. This train ran daily and carried several coffins together with the mourners. This service continued until the Second World War when the station was destroyed in an air raid and was never continued.

On the main line to Basingstoke is 'Battle of Britain' 4–6–2 no. 34077 *603 Squadron*.

At Pirbright there is a junction to the left for Aldershot, well known to many squaddies where they were welcomed to their first taste of Army discipline. On from Pirbright is Sturt Junction with lines leading north and south – north to Ascot and Reading, south going through Aldershot. We are now relaxing again and taking in the scenery, white exhaust drifting past the windows. The shadow of our train on the other line accompanies us in the bright sunshine and all is well with our band of enthusiasts. Through Farnborough, Fleet, Winchfield and Hook, our guess would be in excess of 60mph, and now we feel the brakes being gently applied to bring our speed down in preparation for our stop at Basingstoke. And here we are, doors bang and the station announcer tells everyone this train is for Bournemouth – not that we shall have time to leave the train as we shall only stop for a very short time. With a gentle jerk, we are under way again.

'Merchant Navy' 4–6–2 SR no. 21C12 *United States Line* in original form heads a Pullman Bournemouth express through Basingstoke in 1947.

'Merchant Navy' 4–6–2 no. 35030 *Elder Dempster Lines* works its way through Basingstoke with 'The Bournemouth Belle'.

With a Railway Correspondence and Travel Society special at Basingstoke, is 'Merchant Navy' no. 35011 *General Steam Navigation*.

Almost from the end of Basingstoke station there is a junction on the left that leads to Fareham and Gosport, where a ferry operates to the Isle of Wight. Photographed with a Bournemouth express at Basingstoke is 'King Arthur' class 4–6–0 no. 30805 *Sir Constantine*.

The junction to Fareham that has been mentioned meanders its way southwards via Alton where there is a junction with the line from Guildford making its way westwards. On this line is Medstead and Alresford. The Fareham line continues southward via Droxford.

Medstead station, not far from Alton on the Guildford–Winchester line.

M7 no. 30378, a Drummond design of 1897 for the L&SWR at Alresford.

A loco with a very long life, 0–6–0T AIX no. 32646 at Droxford station, built in 1872 by Stroudley for the LB&SCR.

Just before Fareham there is a junction to the right which heads for Eastleigh; off this line is a short branch heading north to Bishop's Waltham opened in 1863 for the L&SWR. Here is class C14 0–4–0T no. 30589, originally introduced in 1906 to a Drummond design as a 2–2–0T motor train. It was rebuilt by Urie in 1923 as an 0–4–0T shunting engine.

M7 0–4–4T no. 30054 photographed in 1952 on a very wet day in Fareham station.

In much better weather is this view of U class 2–6–0 no. 31639, again in Fareham station.

While we have been talking about the line to Fareham and looking at some pictures on that route, our train has been making progress towards a well-known location for railway enthusiasts and photographers, where our train for Bournemouth will part company with the main line for Salisbury and the West Country – the famous Battledown flyover.

'West Country' 4–6–2 no. 34027 *Taw Valley* leans to the curve at Battledown with a Plymouth train. The flyover dominates the scene.

Both of these views of Battledown and the flyover were taken on the same day,
8 September 1952.

S15 4–6–0 no. 30832 passing under the huge ironwork of the flyover.

An H15, this time no. 30487, photographed with the flyover in the background.

We are past Battledown and on our way to our next major location, Eastleigh works and shed. After slowing for the major junction at Battledown we are now picking up speed again. The next station we shall pass through will be Micheldever. There will be little time to see anything there, so we can stay in our seats and build up our energies for Eastleigh, check our cameras – all railway enthusiasts constantly check their equipment – set focus exposures, etc. just in case they have to grab the camera and make sure they don't miss a picture. The next station will be Winchester, and then the excitement will rise as we collect our shoulder bags with our notebooks. Our cameras will of course be carried in our hands, as we shall soon be into Eastleigh station where we leave our train and make our way to the sheds and works.

S15 4–6–0 no. 30502 near Winchester.

B4 0–4–0T no. 30082 shunts at Winchester. With driving wheels of only 3ft 9in, and tractive effort of over 14,000lbs, these locos were ideal for working small yards and docks.

On the main line near Winchester are two views of 'King Arthurs' on their way to Bournemouth via Southampton.

'King Arthur' class NI5 no. 30737 *King Uther* near Winchester.

At the same spot NI5 'King Arthur' no. 30743 *Lyonesse*.

Photographed near Shawford is Bulleid 4–6–2 'Battle of Britain' no. 34090 which has the longest nameplate of any of the class: *Sir Eustace Missenden Southern Railway*. It is only a short distance from here to Eastleigh.

Once again our train is slowing for the stop at Eastleigh. We are standing near the door ready to detrain and make our way to Eastleigh works, clutching our passes to visit the works and shed. Eastleigh station was opened in 1839 for the London & Southampton Railway. As with so many other stations it was designed by Sir William Tite. It was extended in 1895 by the L&SWR and was known as Bishopstoke until 1889, being renamed Eastleigh at the start of the twentieth century. Eastleigh was a railway town, with an enlarged station and a large works. The works were completed in 1909 by the L&SWR, covering over 40 acres, and the first locomotives to emerge were a couple of S14 0–4–0Ts. By the grouping in 1923 over 300 locomotives had been built at the works. Many notable designs have been built including 'Lord Nelsons', 'Schools', 'Merchant Navies' and 'West Countries'. During the Second World War much war work was undertaken including anti-aircraft guns and assault craft. There is still a lot of work carried out here on steam engines, including rebuilding the Bulleids.

T9 4–4–0 no. 30702 leaving Eastleigh station with a stopping train to Southampton.

While we are making our way to Eastleigh works, a 'Lord Nelson' goes through Eastleigh station non-stop on its way to Southampton Central and Bournemouth. This view is of no. 30865 *Sir John Hawkins* on the central road at Eastleigh.

It takes about 10 minutes to walk to the works and shed from the station. The walk is very close to the lines through Eastleigh station, so our ears are tuned to listen for any train going past. We did not have to wait very long – a few minutes after leaving the station a 'Merchant Navy' with a Bournemouth express roared past.

'Merchant Navy' no. 35008 *Orient Line* passing through Eastleigh station.

Clutching our passes ready to present to the guardian of the works, the excitement is growing as we near the entrance. There seem to be locos everywhere, the cameras are already being used, taking general views for our records. We have already been given details about the works from one of our friends, but talking about it in the confines of a compartment on a train does not adequately prepare you for the size. Here we are at the entrance and we are given a cheery greeting, tinged with the usual 'why on earth do you want to go around here?'
We are given a suitable guide, and we are off on a works tour.

'Lord Nelson' 4–6–0 no. 30865 *Sir John Hawkins* undergoing overhaul in the works in 1956.

Like all works, unless you have complete freedom to go anywhere, good photography is very difficult with so many posts and pillars in the way. What looks to us like debris is all part of the skills of the workers as they know where every bit of 'debris' goes. Outside is a different story, with locos that have emerged from the paint shops looking brand new!

An O2 0–4–4T of 1889 vintage, looking brand new outside Eastleigh works. Behind is an unidentified 'Schools' class.

Q class 0–6–0 no. 30549, a much later design of 1938 by Maunsell, sporting a rather unsuitable stovepipe chimney. This was later changed to a multiple jet blastpipe and large chimney, which made it look like a much more powerful engine.

Two more ex-works locos in the yard at Eastleigh.

'Schools' class 4–4–0 no. 30913 *Christ's Hospital* in the early 1950s.

Another spotless engine turned out from Eastleigh works after overhaul – Z class 0–8–0T no. 30953.

'Lord Nelson' class 4–6–0 no. 30850 *Lord Nelson* outside Eastleigh works in May 1961.

In the early days at Eastleigh is this view of LB&SCR Atlantic no. 32037 *Selsey Bill*, believed to have been photographed in 1948.

'Remembrance' N15X class no. 32329 *Stephenson* in early Southern Region years at Eastleigh.

Our visit to Eastleigh works and sheds is nearly over now. Our notebooks are full, and cameras have been well used. We shall soon be parting company with our guide who has been very helpful and informative, and we will have to make our way back to Eastleigh station where we shall catch a train to Southampton and on to Bournemouth.

'Merchant Navy' 4–6–2 no. 35019 *French Line C.G.T.*, one of the engines chosen for the 1948 exchange trials. It is seen here at Eastleigh coupled to an LMS tender which held more water than its own tender.

C14 0–4–0T no. 30588 first saw service in 1906 attached to a carriage as a motor train, but was rebuilt as a shunting engine in 1923.

Back at Eastleigh station we take the opportunity to visit the refreshment room to stock up on food and drinks.

M7 no. 30049 waiting to depart Eastleigh station with a local stopping train.

Two views of 'The Bournemouth Belle' non-stop through Eastleigh station. 'Lord Nelsons'
were used on this service until the outbreak of the Second World War when the service was
suspended. It was resumed in October 1946 but was headed by the new 'Merchant Navies'
hauling ten Pullman cars instead of the pre-war seven.

'Merchant Navy' 4–6–2 no. 35015 *Rotterdam Lloyd* speeds 'The Bournemouth Belle' through Eastleigh.

Another unrebuilt 'Merchant Navy' no. 35021 *New Zealand Line* also on 'The Bournemouth Belle' at
Eastleigh.

Our train for Bournemouth has arrived and our luck is in as we find an empty compartment.
On our way again, we will be going through Swaythling and St Denys, and just after Northam
there is a junction for Southampton docks.

'USA' class 0–6–0T no. 30064, introduced in 1942 for the US Army Transport Corps. These locos were
purchased from the USA in 1946 for working Southampton docks.

Three more views of steam in the docks area. The 'USA' tanks seem to dominate the scene.

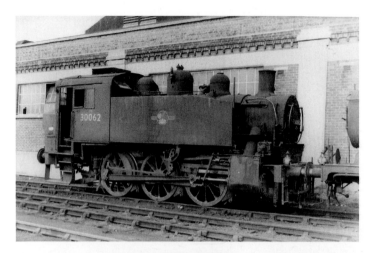

'USA' 0–6–0 no. 30062 in the sidings at Southampton docks.

E4 0–6–2T no. 32491 also in Southampton docks, photographed at the same location as the view above.

'USA' no. 30072 shunting in the docks.

Southampton, or Clausentum as it was called in Roman times, was an important port, bringing supplies to their soldiers stationed in Britain, and also trade goods. When the Romans left, the Saxons took over and by the Middle Ages it had developed to such a degree that it was almost as important as Bristol and London. In the sixteenth century it became a major trading post. Amid the threat of invasion by Napoleon, major works were put in hand to develop Southampton. In 1803, the first docks were built, and in 1831 the Southampton London Branch Railway and Dock Company arrived. Further rebuilding took place over the years, and in 1932 the docks were enlarged to take much larger ships.

'Merchant Navy' 4–6–2 no. 35017 *Belgian Marine* preparing to leave Southampton docks with a Boat Special to Waterloo. It is carrying a headboard 'Holland America', so presumably it's carrying passengers from the USA to the English capital.

We shall be staying on our train to Bournemouth, but while we have been talking about Southampton docks, several of our band of enthusiasts have been telling us about their experiences on the Isle of Wight, so I propose to sit back on the cushions, have a sandwich and give the floor to them. Their trips to the island started on joining the ferry in Southampton docks to Ryde on the Isle of Wight. On arrival, the train service from Ryde appeared to be pure Southern Railway with O2 0–4–4T working the trains built for the L&SWR by Adams in 1889. A number of the class were transferred to the Isle of Wight at the grouping in 1923. They were fitted with Westinghouse Brakes and the coal bunkers were enlarged. There were originally three companies running the service on the island: the Isle of Wight Central Railway, which was an amalgamation of three earlier railways; the Isle of Wight Eastern Section and the Isle of Wight Newport Junction Railway.

Isle of Wight O2 0–4–4T no. W15 *Cowes* photographed at Ventnor, showing the entrance to the tunnel that the Earl of Yarborough forced the Isle of Wight Eastern Section to build to avoid his property.

In 1890 the Isle of Wight became an independent administrative county. Regular visitors Queen Victoria and Prince Albert would arrive by train at Gosport on their way to Osborne House, their private home on the island.

Class E1 0–6–0T no. W2 *Yarmouth*, photographed at Wroxall on the Isle of Wight. Built for the LB&SCR in 1874 by Stroudley, it was rebuilt by Marsh before finding its way to the Isle of Wight when the Southern Railway became responsible for the island's railways.

W22 *Brading*
photographed at Brading
in 1954.

W21 *Sandown*, an O2
0–4–4T, leaving Ryde.

W14 *Fishbourne*, another
O2, regrettably at an
unknown station on the
Isle of Wight.

We discussed the Southampton docks in our compartment, particularly the 'USA' tanks which appear rather alien to most of us, especially, if like me, you come from the West Country where the GWR thought it was a crime to have pipework and bits and pieces outside of the frames in view of the public. We shall soon be into Southampton Central, where we stop for a few minutes – time to stretch our legs and perhaps get a nice picture of the loco at the head of our train.

Many Standard class locos were shedded in the Southampton and Bournemouth areas, and also for working trains such as 'The Pines Express' over the Mendips to Bath. Here, no. 73081 arrives at Southampton Central with a Waterloo–Bournemouth West train.

Another Standard class at Southampton Central, this time no. 76066 which poses alongside 'West Country' no. 34101 *Hartland*.

'West Country' no. 34020 *Seaton* arriving at Southampton station. In the background is 'Merchant Navy' no. 35001 *Channel Packet*.

This time the photograph is taken from a low angle of 'West Country' no. 34038 *Lynton* at Central station.

We are on our way again, pulling out of Southampton Central towards Bournemouth. Almost immediately, if you look towards the left, you will see where the liners berth at the Ocean Terminal. If we are lucky either the *Queen Mary* or the *Queen Elizabeth* will be there, and we are lucky as *Queen Elizabeth* is in dock. We are through Millbrook, and then we come to Redbridge where the line branches to the right for Salisbury and Bristol.

U class 2–6–0 no. 31809 leaving Southampton Central with a Portsmouth–Bristol train.

On through Totton and then comes Lyndhurst Road, soon we shall be into New Forest territory, where we may see some ponies from the carriage windows – although they are a bit nervous of trains. The ponies, however, have a right of way over road users, and woe betide the driver who ignores these rules. After Lyndhurst Road comes Beaulieu and now we are really into the New Forest!

'West Country' no. 34010 *Sidmouth* near Lyndhurst Road.

Beaulieu Road station, opened by the L&SWR in 1847.

'Lord Nelson' class 4–6–0 no. 30858 *Lord Duncan* near Brockenhurst on its way to Bournemouth.

This is what visitors to the New Forest come to see and enjoy, the trees, the atmosphere and above all the ponies. The foal is interested in the camera, but mum and dad are more concerned with filling their stomachs!

Shortly after Brockenhurst comes the junction for Lymington and Holmsley. Lymington has been a port since Roman times. The railway, albeit a single line and only 5 miles long, was completed in 1858 and was very well used, although it did not quite reach the pier where the ferry left for the Isle of Wight. This situation continued until 1884 when the L&SWR extended the line to the quayside. This proved very popular with travellers with a number of trains running daily direct to Lymington from Waterloo. The junction to Holmsley goes through Ringwood and then at West Moors there is a junction for Salisbury. The main line leads on to Poole and Dorchester, bypassing Bournemouth.

'Lord Nelson' no. 30865 *Sir John Hawkins* crossing Holmsley Heath on its way to Bournemouth with a train from Waterloo.

After the junction to Lymington, we continue to admire the view through the windows, through Sway, then New Milton, an area I remember well from my childhood. My father was stationed at RAF Holmsley, and we moved to New Milton in 1944. My lasting memory of the New Forest was lines of tanks and lorries with thousands of soldiers, mostly Americans who were handing out chocolate and chewing gum to all the children in large quantities. Of course we knew nothing about an invasion force, which of course it was; it was just very exciting to us.

U class 2–6–0 no. 31808 near New Milton.

H15 class 4–6–0 no. 30489, an early design by Urie for the L&SWR in 1914, photographed near New Milton.

Another view at the same spot. Both trains are heading for Bournemouth. This is of U class no. 31632.

We are starting the usual preparations for our arrival at Bournemouth as we are given some facts about the town by one of our friends. Before the arrival of the railway, Bournemouth hardly qualified as a village, with a population of less than 200. The original route of the railway from Southampton was via Ringwood and Dorchester, completely bypassing Bournemouth, whose residents continued a quiet, uneventful life. All this was about to change. Bournemouth got its name from a stream called the Bourne, which ran through the centre of the village, and where locals collected their water. The rather well-off residents began to enjoy the smell of the pine forest which surrounded Bournemouth, and the waters were said to be beneficial to health, so a resort emerged and by the 1860s the population had grown to nearly 6,000. At last it was worthwhile to build a railway to the town and the first company to do so was the Ringwood, Christchurch & Bournemouth Railway, but the station they built at Bournemouth was still a half-hour walk from the centre, and was a ramshackle affair, not approved of by the residents and visitors. Finally the L&SWR woke up and a direct line from Southampton via Christchurch and Pokesdown was opened in 1888. Also, a fine new station was built, albeit still not in the centre, but it was at least called Bournemouth Central. At last the fastest-growing resort was served by a railway direct from Waterloo.

'Merchant Navy' no. 35029 *Ellerman Lines* prepares to leave Bournemouth Central with a Waterloo-bound train.

M7 0–4–4T no. 30104 station pilot at Bournemouth Central.

I am not very conversant with the Southern Region's code system, but looking at a book that tells me where the train or loco is heading, shows that this train should be nowhere near Bournemouth. However, despite the codes, it is heading a Weymouth train out of Bournemouth. It is headed by N class 2–6–0 no. 31859. In the background is the shed yard.

A B4 0–4–0T no. 30087 weighing in at only 33 tons, built by Adams for shunting. This class of locos was used principally for dock shunting in the 1890s. They were to be seen at Southampton and at many more of the L&SWR's harbourside and docks areas in the early part of the twentieth century. This view is in Bournemouth shed yard in July 1954.

'West Country' 4–6–2 no. 34108 *Wincanton* on Bournemouth shed.

Standard class 2–6–4T 4MT no. 80081 alongside 'Merchant Navy' no. 35014 *Nederland Line* ready for duty on Bournemouth shed.

Waterloo-bound; two views of Pacific locos about to leave Bournemouth Central.

'Britannia' 4–6–2 no. 70009 *Alfred the Great* about to head for the capital with 'The Bournemouth Belle'.

'West Country' 4–6–2 no. 34006 *Bude*. This was one of the Southern Region engines to take part in the 1948 exchanges. Working on the Western, it ran Exeter–Bristol, and on the Eastern Region it worked out of Marylebone to Leicester, and did all that was asked of it!

Leaving Bournemouth Central for Bournemouth West and on to Weymouth is 'West Country' 4–6–2 no. 34102 *Lapford*.

Bournemouth West, the final destination for the Somerset & Dorset Joint Railway from Bath. Trains from the north, such as Bradford and Sheffield, came into the terminus at Bath where a fresh engine would be coupled up to what was the last coach in the train, which now became the lead coach. On leaving Bath for Bournemouth, there is a steep climb to Combe Down tunnel at 1 in 50; the line then eases for a while until just after Radstock where there is a further 3 miles at 1 in 50 followed by another steep climb to Masbury Summit, and then a descent at 1 in 50 to Evercreech. The line continues to be a bit up and down until arriving in Bournemouth West.

With L&SWR on the tender, 4–4–0 no. 568 waits in the yard at Bournemouth West, probably waiting to work a train back to Bournemouth and possibly Southampton.

Somerset & Dorset Joint Railway no. 45 is ready to leave Bournemouth West with a train for Bath.

An early view at Bournemouth West is this picture of Somerset & Dorset Joint Railway 4–4–0 no. 67 in 1920.

Another view at Bournemouth West. This time Somerset & Dorset Joint Railway no. 19 is posed in the yard. The driver and fireman are happy to smile for the camera in this summer view, 1925.

On from Bournemouth West is Branksome, Parkstone and Poole, and then comes Wareham and a branch to Corfe and Swanage, a picturesque line with Corfe Castle towering above the station at Corfe.

M7 no. 30027 at Wareham with a Swanage train.

End of the branch line to Swanage. This is a view of the one-road shed and turntable at Swanage.

It's getting near to the end of the Bournemouth part of this journey and we shall soon head back to Battledown flyover, this time taking the main line to the west. For the last couple of pictures we will visit Dorchester and Weymouth.

'West Country' no. 34041 *Wilton* between Wareham and Dorchester.

O2 class no. 30231 at Dorchester in 1952.

From Dorchester the line turns south going through a lovely little station in a cutting called Upwey Wishing Well Halt. Shortly after is a junction to the right and a 6-mile long branch (originally a GWR line opened in 1885) to the lovely village of Abbotsbury. At Abbotsbury is an ancient monastery and one somewhat unusual tourist attraction is a large swannery. Back on the main line and several miles further on is Weymouth.

Class O2 0–4–4T no. 30230, an Adams design for the L&SWR, at Abbotsbury.

'Merchant Navy' no. 35005 *Canadian Pacific* on Weymouth shed.

We have now finished the Waterloo–Bournemouth part of this journey, so it is time to make our way back to Basingstoke to catch a train for Salisbury and the West Country.

'Merchant Navy' no. 35009 *Shaw Savill* arriving at Basingstoke in 1958.

A view of 'King Arthur' class 4–6–0 no. SR 798 *Sir Hectimere* near Battledown with a train to Southampton in 1937.

In 1947 the Southern Railway introduced a new all-Pullman service from Waterloo, 'The Devon Belle'. Originally it was to serve travellers to Ilfracombe, but very quickly a portion of Pullmans was added that would be detached at Exeter and taken on to Plymouth. A beavertail observation coach was also added, making the train up to fourteen coaches and weighing nearly 550 tons – an enormous load to work over the gradients west of Salisbury. Another unique feature of this train was the watering arrangements. It ran non-stop through Salisbury, and stopped at Wilton to take water. 'The Devon Belle' would detach four coaches at Exeter, but it was still a heavy train. On the final few miles to Ilfracombe is the steepest gradient on a British main line – the 1 in 36 at Mortehoe – and a banking engine was always required. 'The Devon Belle' was withdrawn in 1952 owing to a lack of passengers.

'The Devon Belle' with 'Merchant Navy' no. 35012 *United States Line* at its head.

From Battledown, it's not far to Andover but first comes Hurstbourne with its junction to Redbridge and St Denys. A few more miles after Hurstbourne and we shall be into Andover where we shall stop for several minutes – we may even have time to stock up on refreshments!

Class U1 2–6–0 no. 31904 near Andover with a train from Southampton.

'West Country' no. 34023 *Blackmore Vale* with a train for Plymouth, at Andover.

'Lord Nelson' 4–6–0 no. 30860 *Lord Hawke* at Andover.

Two 'Merchant Navy' class engines at Andover, both on Plymouth trains. Both photographs were taken on the same day, 20 June 1950.

'Merchant Navy' no. 35001 *Channel Packet* picking up passengers at Andover.

Another 'Merchant Navy' at Andover; this time it's no. 35003 *Royal Mail*.

20 June 1950 was a busy day for steam at Andover. Here are two more views.

'King Arthur' class 4–6–0 no. 30452 *Sir Meliagrance*.

Another 'King Arthur', no. 30455 *Sir Launcelot*, again stopped for passengers at Andover.

'The Atlantic Coast Express', or the ACE as it was known to enginemen and loco spotters, was a multi-portioned train with coaches for Ilfracombe, Plymouth, Torrington, Bude and finally Padstow. The kitchen cars were detached at Exeter and there was also a coach for Exmouth and Sidmouth. With all these holiday destinations, I would have thought 'The Atlantic Coast Holiday Express' would have been more appropriate. Introduced by the Southern Railway in 1926, it left Waterloo at 11a.m. and ran 84 miles non-stop to Salisbury. After Salisbury, high speeds were run, often approaching the 90s as drivers liked to have some time in hand before Seaton Bank which, for 7 miles, varied between 1 in 80 and 1 in 130, then through Honiton tunnel and down to Exeter Central. Here, coaches were detached for the various holiday destinations while the main portion to Plymouth had three other coaches added. At Okehampton, the Bude and Padstow portions were detached and the remaining coaches finished their journey in Plymouth. In the reverse direction 'The Atlantic Coast Express' left Padstow at 8.40 a.m.

'The Atlantic Coast Express' with 'Merchant Navy' no. 35024 *East Asiatic Company* carrying the ACE headboard.

Salisbury's first railway was really classed as a branch line from Bishopstoke (Eastleigh) opened in 1847. The first station was Salisbury Milford although it was only used as the main station for about ten years, until the L&SWR joined the Salisbury and Yeovil Railway and the present station opened 1859. The station, when first opened, only had one platform until a second was added for London-bound trains a few years later. In 1900 a complete rebuild took place and new platforms were added. Salisbury Cathedral is a tourist attraction, and has many visitors in the summer months. The cathedral was built on a most unlikely site for such a huge building, Salisbury Water Meadows. Building took place in the thirteenth century, and 100 years later, its spire was added, making it the tallest in England. The artist John Constable painted the cathedral in 1823.

Sunshine and snow at Salisbury. In lovely summer sunshine, 'West Country' 4–6–2 no. 34023 *Blackmore Vale* leaves Salisbury for Waterloo.

In totally different conditions is this view of 'West Country' no. 34035 *Shaftesbury* in the depths of winter in 1963.

Three views at the east end of Salisbury station.

M7 4–4–0T no. 30673 station pilot at Salisbury.

Z class no. 30957, a Maunsell design of 1929 for heavy shunting, works a transfer freight through Salisbury station.

'Merchant Navy' no. 35024 *East Asiatic Company*, at the head of a Plymouth–Waterloo train, starts its heavy load out of Salisbury.

S15 class 4–6–0 no. 30499 in Salisbury shed yard.

Another view in Salisbury yard is of 'West Country' no. 34099 *Lynmouth*.

Also in Salisbury shed yard is another S15, no. 30831.

4–4–0 no. 30398 on Salisbury shed with an empty tender. It has probably just come on shed from working a train.

Another view on shed, no. 31626 in 1962.

Plymouth-bound 'Merchant Navy' 4–6–2 no. 35004 *Cunard White Star* awaits clear signals at Salisbury. When it gets the green light we shall all be at the windows as the main line runs right past Salisbury shed 72B and a clear view is had of any locos in the yard.

Leaving Salisbury for the west, the Southern line runs parallel with the GWR line that heads north to Westbury as far as Wilton where we curve left for the West Country. Not long after parting company, we pass near Stonehenge, one of Britain's major heritage sites, known to date back to 300 BC. It is believed to have been a place of worship for Pagans and then Druids. Some of the stones weigh in excess of 40 tons. The summer solstice has been celebrated at Stonehenge since the 1870s.

Stonehenge – enjoyed by children as well as adults.

'West Country' class no. 34014 *Budleigh Salterton* having brought a train in from Brighton via Southampton to Salisbury, makes its way from the station to Salisbury shed.

We are on our way westwards now. It is about 28 miles to Templecombe and I am informed that there will not be much to see over this stretch of line except pleasant countryside. It's time to relax and enjoy the sound of our engine working hard, smoke drifting past the window, the clicking of the rail joints, the sun shining – what more could a group of railway enthusiasts want? Our next stop will be Templecombe where we will cross the Somerset and Dorset line. The line heads north through Wincanton and on to Bath, while south goes through Sturminster Newton and eventually to Bournemouth West. In the Second World War a German aircraft dumped its bombs which hit the Templecombe station area, killing thirteen people.

Sturminster Newton station was opened in 1863 by the Somerset & Dorset Joint Railway.

Rebuilt 'West Country' no. 34026 *Yes Tor* approaching Templecombe with a Plymouth-bound freight.

We are now through Templecombe. We did manage a couple of photographs, nothing wonderful, although they will no doubt bring back memories when we look at the finished prints in the future. After Templecombe, we are expecting fireworks from our engine, as speeds well in excess of 80mph are normal at Milbourne and Sherbourne, before slowing for our stop at Yeovil Junction. The station is several miles from Yeovil Town station, so there is usually a local with an M7 waiting to convey passengers from Junction Station to Yeovil Town.

M7 no. 30129 photographed at Yeovil Junction.

'Merchant Navy' 4–6–2 no. 35022 *Holland America Line* preparing to leave Yeovil Junction.

M7 0–4–4T no. 30021 arriving at Yeovil Town. There is a small shed at Yeovil Town which is easily seen from the station – the entrance is from the Down platform.

On the main line near Yeovil is 'Lord Nelson' no. 30865 *Sir John Hawkins*.

After Yeovil comes another fairly long part of our journey. Leaving Yeovil we shall once again be picking up speed, first comes Sutton Bingham then Crewkerne, where our speed will be over 60mph, and Chard Junction where our speed will still be rising, and then to Axminster. We seem to be going very fast with our group wildly estimating our speed, even 100mph was guessed, but after looking at various logs by experts I think 80mph was more realistic.

Class 0415 no. 30583, a 4–4–2T built by Adams for the L&SWR. In 1882 these locos were used on the branch line from Axminster to Lyme Regis, photographed at Axminster.

S15 4–6–0 no. 30823, a Urie design for the L&SWR in 1920 with only 5ft 7in wheels. They were used as mixed traffic locos and this view is at Axminster with an Exeter train.

'Merchant Navy' 4–6–2 no. 35014 *Nederland Line* near Axminster. How the crew can see where they are going is a mystery, the amount of smoke suggests they are burning some very poor quality coal or the fireman is not up to the job.

Speeding through Axminster is 'Merchant Navy' no. 35009 *Shaw Savill*.

From Axminster is a branch to Lyme Regis, worked for many years by the 0415 class 4–4–2T. Lyme Regis is a quiet harbour on the south coast, a favourite with holiday-makers. It was at Lyme Regis in 1685 that the Duke of Monmouth arrived by ship, and started the Monmouth Rebellion. Lyme Regis is also famous for its fossils. The cliffs along the shore frequently collapse and expose many fossils from 185 million years ago. Lyme Regis and the cliffs in the area are known as the Jurassic Coast. Most days, people can be seen turning over rocks looking for that special fossil!

Another of the 0415 class, no. 30584, at Lyme Regis with a train from Axminster. During the summer months these 4–4–2T locos are busy with trains full of holiday-makers.

0415 no. 30582 with a summer holiday train at Lyme Regis.

A final view at Lyme Regis before we continue westwards. This time it's 0415 no. 30583 on a lovely summer's day.

After Axminster it is only a short distance to Seaton Junction where there is another branch line to a holiday destination, Seaton. Our speed will drop a little to about 60mph. Here, 'King Arthur' class no. 746 *Pendragon* makes a fine picture as it speeds through Seaton Junction in 1936.

Another fine pre-war view of a King Arthur at Seaton Junction. This time it is no. 451 *Sir Lamorak* speeding through on the centre line.

After Seaton Junction comes Honiton, always an exciting part of the journey as trains plunge into Honiton tunnel. It must be quite an experience to ride the footplate and see the tunnel approaching, suddenly being surrounded by darkness with only the glow of the fire to illuminate the controls. After Honiton is Sidmouth Junction.

Collecting the single line token at Ottery St Mary is 2–6–2T 2MT no. 41306 working an Exeter–Sidmouth holiday train in 1950.

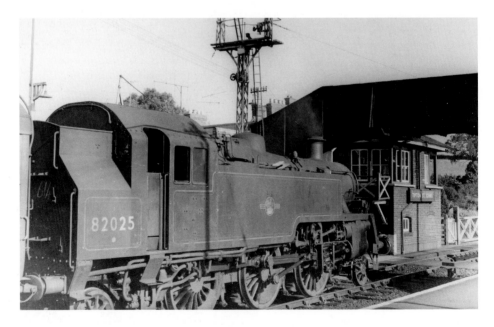

Standard class 3MT 2–6–2T no. 82025 at Tipton St John, where the junction to Sidmouth branches left and leaves the line that continues on to Exmouth.

Class C 0–6–0 no. 31590, introduced in 1900, built by Wainwright for the South Eastern & Chatham Railway near Sidmouth with a train from Exeter.

Sidmouth signal-box. The L&SWR opened the station in 1874, so I think it is safe to guess this box was opened at the same time.

On from Sidmouth comes Whimple, Broadclyst and then we shall start slowing for Pinhoe and our eventual stop in Exeter. Before Exeter is the junction to Exmouth. This is another holiday line but it also sees quite a lot of troop movement as the Royal Marine Commandos have a large base at Lympstone.

0415 4–4–2T no. 30583 with a train for Exmouth.

M7 0–4–4T no. 30045 at Exmouth with a train for Sidmouth Junction.

We are now approaching Exeter, but we must have our cameras ready as we shall pass Exmouth Junction shed on the right, just before Exeter Central station. Very quickly we take up positions by the windows, with cameras ready, as we shall get a good view of the shed which is clearly visible from the main line.

'Battle of Britain' class no. 34051 *Winston Churchill*. The former prime minister is no doubt a worthy recipient of the honour of having such an engine named after him.

'West Country' no. 34013 *Okehampton* prepares to set off from Exeter Central to Waterloo.

Waiting in the central road at Exeter Central is 'Merchant Navy' no. 35018 *British India Line*, carrying the headboard 'Atlantic Coast Express'.

Heading for London with a Plymouth–Waterloo train is 'West Country' no. 34036 *Westward Ho*. Ahead is over 160 miles of hard slog in places, with fast downhill in others. On arrival in Waterloo, the crew feel they have done a good job.

A pre-Second World War view at Exeter Central, M7 no. 356 arrives with a train from Exmouth in the 1920s.

M7 0–4–4 no. 30668 has either just arrived or is ready to depart Exeter Central with an Exmouth train in 1952.

Yet another Exmouth train headed by an M7, no. 30023, waiting in Exeter Central, this time in 1959. The platform looks rather wet, not the holiday weather many passengers were hoping for.

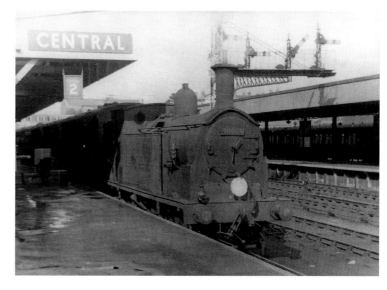

The railways in the Exeter area started as broad gauge. The Exeter & Crediton Railway came
into existence in 1845. The L&SWR owned many shares in the company and wanted the line
built to standard gauge, but it finally opened in 1851 as broad gauge before being leased to the
Bristol & Exeter Railway. By 1876 things had changed again, the L&SWR had taken back the
lease, bought the line and converted it to standard gauge by 1879. The L&SWR also took over
the Exeter & Exmouth Railway in 1866.

0415 no. 30582 at Exmouth Junction in 1959.

Resident on Exmouth Junction shed is Z class 0–8–0T no. 30952, a Maunsell design
of 1929.

Standard class 2–6–2T 3MT no. 82013 on Exmouth shed. These locos were displacing the older Southern Railway engines on the holiday branch lines like Lyme Regis and Exmouth.

Another view of a Standard 2–6–2T 3MT on Exmouth shed, this time no. 82019. This class was introduced in 1952, a Swindon design with 5ft 3in wheels and a tractive effort of over 21,000lbs. They performed admirably on local stoppers and branch lines.

Back at Exeter Central we await the train that will take us on the last leg of our Southern journey that will end in Padstow. There is an N class 2–6–0 waiting in the centre line to take us to our final destination. The train we are waiting for is a Waterloo–Plymouth train which will be divided at Exeter with four coaches being taken over by the 2–6–0 that is patiently waiting. We hear a distant whistle and our train with a 'West Country' in charge comes into view. We watch with interest as the staff divide the train, and of course we take photographs of all the action. We pile into another empty compartment and we are on our way. From Central station to Exeter St Davids the line goes downhill very steeply – one of our team tells us it is one of the steepest in the country, on a par with the Lickey Incline at about 1 in 38.

N class 2–6–0 no. 31831 arriving at Exeter St Davids.

Leaving Exeter behind, we are now in the lush Devon countryside. We shall pass through many towns and villages that have given their names to the 'West Country' class. First will be Crediton although our band of enthusiasts will not be leaving the train until we arrive in Padstow. However, we must mention the branch just after Yeoford that leads to Barnstaple. Through undulating countryside, the journey from Exeter takes about an hour. At Barnstaple Junction there is a branch left to Bideford and Torrington, while the main destination of Ilfracombe is reached by some of the steepest gradients in Britain. There is a 3-mile gradient at 1 in 40, and on the approach to Ilfracombe it steepens to 1 in 36 for over 2 miles.

Torrington viaduct in 1933, between Bideford and Torrington.

M7 0–4–4T no. 42 outside Torrington's tiny shed in 1935.

On from Barnstaple Junction comes Barnstaple Town, from where the Lynton & Barnstaple
Narrow Gauge Railway ran. Opened in May 1898 as a single line, it ran through rugged
countryside until arriving in Lynton – or rather above Lynton, as the station was on the cliff top,
from where visitors were taken by cliff railway down to the harbour and beach area. The line
was never a big financial success and closed in 1935. The line also boasted the largest bridge
on a narrow gauge line in Britain: Chelfham viaduct, built in 1898, with eight arches, being 70ft
high and 133 yards long.

Class E1/R no. 2695 in a Southern Railway view at Barnstaple in the 1930s.

Lynton & Barnstaple no. 8, double-heading a train on the 19-mile journey from
Barnstaple to Lynton.

We are nearly into Cornwall now and getting the feeling that all visitors have when travelling in that lovely county. You are never far from the sea and the air seems cleaner, but we still have a few miles yet to go. Passing through North Tawton, we approach Okehampton. There is a small sub shed which is visible from the train, so we shall be keeping a look-out just in case, and with a squeal of brakes we come to a halt in Okehampton.

2–6–0 no. 31846 arriving at Okehampton with a Bude train.

N class 2–6–0 no. 1828 in Southern Railway days, running light engine through Okehampton, possibly making its way to the small sub shed there.

Okehampton station was opened in 1871 by the Devon & Cornwall Railway then absorbed by the L&SWR.

'Battle of Britain' class no. 34074 *46 Squadron* arriving at Okehampton from Exeter.

Leaving Okehampton, we shortly come to Meldon Junction, where the North Cornwall line and Plymouth line divide. At Meldon there is a high, lattice steel viaduct and at this point we are nearly 1,000ft above sea level, the highest point on the Southern Region rail network.

Meldon Viaduct, clearly showing the intricate lattice work of this structure.

N class 2–6–0 no. 31895 with a Plymouth–Tavistock train.

From Meldon we shall be taking the North Cornwall Line, leaving the main line and heading for our final destination. One of our group who has travelled the main line from Meldon to Plymouth tells us of what we shall be missing. Firstly comes the beauty of Dartmoor, then Bere Alston with its branch line to Callington, then comes Bere Ferrers where you get a view of the Plymouth Waters, before moving on to St Budeaux where passengers get their first view of Brunel's masterpiece, the Royal Albert Bridge at Saltash, built to specific demands by the Royal Navy. It had to be at least 100ft high to give sufficient headroom for their sailing ships. Shortly after seeing the bridge, we arrive in to Plymouth.

Class 757 0–6–2T no. 758 *Lord St Levan*, built in 1907 for the Plymouth, Devonport & South Western Junction Railway, photographed at Callington in 1935. Callington station was opened in 1908.

With a background of Dartmoor is 'Battle of Britain' 4–6–2 no. 34061 *73 Squadron* nearing the end of its journey to Plymouth from Waterloo.

Near Plymouth is 'West Country' no. 34030 *Watersmeet*.

'Battle of Britain' no. 34080 *74 Squadron* working through Plymouth Devonport with a freight train.

Two views taken on Plymouth shed 72D.

Class 757 0–6–2T no. 30757 *Earl of Mount Edgcumbe*.

An ancient 0–4–0T class B4 no. 30089 built in 1891 to an Adams design, especially for working docks areas.

Plymouth, a place steeped in naval history. A Bronze Age settlement was founded here a long time ago although it didn't start to grow as a port until Norman times. By the sixteenth century it was a major port and dock. It is believed that Sir Francis Drake was playing bowls on Plymouth Hoe, before seeing to a little matter of the Spanish Armada coming to attack England, and in 1620 the Pilgrim Fathers set sail from here to form a colony in the New World (America). Plymouth continued to grow and become a major naval base, and in the Second World War was a prime target for German bombers. Extensive damage was caused to the civilian population as destruction of the centre area was almost complete. The docks and the railway system also suffered badly. No doubt the German bombers tried to bring down Brunel's bridge at Saltash, but fortunately for railway enthusiasts, they did not succeed.

N class 2–6–0 no. 31847 standing in Plymouth North Road station with a train from Exeter.

After our chat about the main line that takes travellers to Plymouth, we continue our journey to Padstow. At Meldon we branch right for Halwill Junction, where the line for Bideford leaves us, originally operated by the North Devon & Cornwall Junction Light Railway, and then the L&SWR. The route is rather roundabout but very picturesque.

Watergate Halt opened in July 1925. This was one of many small halts to be found on this line.

Another line that branches at Halwill is for Bude, the North Cornwall resort. Opened by the L&SWR in 1898, the line was built to serve the fishing industry at first, but Bude quickly became a holiday destination.

Southern Railway 4–4–0 no. 170 being serviced at Bude's small engine shed in the 1930s.

We really are getting near the end of our journey. Tired we may be, as railway enthusiasts we have had a wonderful trip and between us we have taken hundreds of photographs, many of locos we have not seen before. No doubt we shall be talking about our railway adventure for months to come, comparing photographs and boasting a little to other enthusiasts not lucky enough to be with us. For now we just sit back, relax and enjoy the last part of our journey. From Halwill we head south to Launceston, Camelford and Wadebridge.

Class O2 0–4–4T no. 203 in Southern colours at Bodmin L&SWR station in the 1930s.

I must admit I have never really given much thought to the name Wadebridge, but one of our informed friends tells us that the town is built near the mouth of the River Camel, and originally there were dwellings either side of the river. The only way to cross from one side to the other was to wait for low tide and wade across. In the fifteenth century there was great concern about the number of people drowning, so a bridge was built and the locals called it Wadebridge. In 1646 Oliver Cromwell with 500 dragoons attacked and seized the bridge during the Civil War. The Wadebridge–Wenford branch opened in 1834 with the sole purpose of transporting sand for the local farming community. The first engine was called *Camel* and the second was named by the makers *Elephant* because they thought *Camel* was referencing the animal, not the river.

'Battle of Britain' class 4–6–2 no. 34065 *Hurricane* arriving at Wadebridge with a train from Padstow to Exeter.

'West Country' no. 340033 *Chard* light engine at Wadebridge.

O2 0–4–4T no. 30193 also on Wadebridge shed, photographed in 1957.

Eighty years after being built, well tank no. 30586 is still at work on the Wadebridge–Wenford branch.

O2 class no. 30200, a 4–4–0 for working local services. This view is at Wadebridge as it works a local to Bodmin.

0–4–4T class O2 no. 30236 storms out of Wadebridge with a train for Bodmin in 1958.

T9 4–4–0 no. 30708 prepares to leave Padstow for Okehampton. It has been a long journey, our Southern adventure. Waterloo seems a long way away as we have travelled through Southampton, Bournemouth and Weymouth, and then taken the main line to the West Country through Salisbury, Exeter, Plymouth and finally through to our destination in Cornwall – Padstow.

Padstow has a long history as a fishing village dating back as far as AD 500, probably existing before even that, perhaps being home to a Stone Age settlement. One of the first recorded events was when a Welsh missionary settled in 'Petroc-Stowe' as Padstow was called in those days. A monastery was built and life was pleasant until the Vikings arrived and disturbed the peace. In 1899 the L&SWR built a station here with a line to Bodmin, originally built as a service to a busy fishing port. However, like so many of these pretty fishing villages, with the coming of the railway the tourist industry boomed and Padstow even had its own named express 'The Atlantic Coast Express' from Waterloo, travelling 260 miles. Padstow also had the distinction of being the end of the line for the L&SWR as it went no further west. We are now within a couple of miles of the terminus at Padstow. From the other compartments we can hear children full of excitement, shouting out 'are we there yet?'. No doubt they are dreaming of building sandcastles on the glorious beaches in the Padstow area, watching the boats in the harbour and eating copious amounts of sweets and cream teas. We hear the squeal of brakes and we come to a halt at the end of our long journey. We leave our train and make our way to the large hotel that overlooks the station. The sun is setting and there is a smell of fish in the air, as we have to pass the sheds where the fishing boats land their catches. There is much activity as many of the local fishermen prepare their boats for a night's fishing. When they come back in the morning, much of their catch will be loaded on a train and despatched to London. We, however are tired after our rail tour, but no doubt we shall be talking about our journey over our evening meal.
I hope you have enjoyed our Southern journey.

Children building sandcastles on Harlyn Bay beach near Padstow.

A Cornish sunset.